OUTREACH
SAVING OUR YOUTH

JOHN 3:16
(Through Effective Christian Witnessing)

DR. MARY "MAY" LARRY, Ph.D.

WESTBOW
PRESS®
A DIVISION OF THOMAS NELSON
& ZONDERVAN

WestBow Press books may be ordered through booksellers or by contacting:

WestBow Press
A Division of Thomas Nelson & Zondervan
1663 Liberty Drive
Bloomington, IN 47403
www.westbowpress.com
844-714-3454

Scripture quotations from the King James Version of the Bible.

ISBN: 978-1-6642-1464-4 (sc)
ISBN: 978-1-6642-1465-1 (e)

Library of Congress Control Number: 2020923637

Print information available on the last page.

WestBow Press rev. date: 12/08/2020

Dedication

This book is dedicated to those who have and continue to partner with love with making and helping me to live my God given destiny. I have realized family is a purposeful strategy from God to evoke and identify the quality of the leader dwelling within. I dedicate this book with love to my granddaughter, Ms. Phoenix- Rosa Erika Parchman-Lee, who I love more than the stars in the sky. Who has consistently given me joy and laughter!

And my son Nathan Louis Lee. My 'Magnificent Angel,' greatest legacy and delight, Nathan Lee, who is a graduate of Columbia University, Chicago. —

And to my best friend and brother, the late Tommie (Tom) Larry, Jr.

You both have always been right here with me, applauding and encouraging me with that brilliant smile. Thank You!

To all my family, friends, and church members. Thank you for always seeing and supporting the leader in me.

Contents

Preface

As one introduced to our Lord Jesus Christ through an outreach ministry, I am writing this book to stress to every reader the importance of this kind of ministry. In order for the reader to gain a better understanding of me as the writer of this book, and the reason why I believe that every believer and saint of God should have a copy or two of this book, allow me to give a portion of my personal testimony on outreach.

It was through outreach that I accepted Jesus Christ as my personal Savior. It seems as if it happened yesterday, even though it has been twenty-eight years. Everything took place at the park on 5th Avenue in Maywood, Illinois, and Miracle Revival Center, between 7:00 and 7:30 p.m. on August 10, 1978. I was working my first summer job as an assistant secretary for the former Mayor of Maywood. One day, I ran into an old friend named Debra, and she began to tell me about a man named Jesus who was full of love and compassion.

As she spoke, I lost all sense of where I was, and I began to weep like a baby as I was encompassed by Jesus' love and compassion. After the experience, I was driven by a thirst for more knowledge about Jesus and His love. My friend picked me up from work the next day so that we could continue our conversation about Jesus. On our way to church that evening, we were faced with many, many obstacles, but PRAISE GOD WE MADE IT. I am saved today, and I know now that God Almighty ordained, ordered, and purposed everything I experienced.

In the early 1960's in Lexington, Mississippi, a young couple had three children and a miscarriage on the fourth child. During the next pregnancy, I was conceived, created for God's use for this time and hour. I have worked in nearly every facet of the church: singing in the choir, counselor, phone counselor, nurse, cook, altar worker, prison ministry, grant-writer, and missionary.

My focus and heart are to work with Outreach ministry, with door-to-door witnessing. I can recall when as a teenager in college, a group of us young women started a club called Alpha Saint Omega. Our purpose was to reach the unsaved and bring them to Christ. I am currently a community Commissioner, Local President Illinois Midwest Ecclesiastical Jurisdiction C.O.G.I.C Business & Professional Women's Federation and the Vice-President of the National Church of God In Christ Business & Professional Women's Federation C.O.G.I.C. Worldwide.

Outreach ministry has been the call and purpose of my life. Please join me as I continue to reach out to our lost and hurting youth and draw them with God's love and compassion.

Dr. Mary "May" Larry, Ph.D.
Author

Introduction

In this world of sin, turmoil, and strife, much attention should be directed toward the interest of our troubled youth. Therefore, I have written this book, *Outreach: Saving Our Youth.* This is a spiritual attempt to address and curtail the mounting problems facing our youth that often lead to family breakdowns, and thus, the communities we all live in. Our young people are faced with gangs, gang-related activity, school violence, and sexual promiscuity on a continual basis. Violence transcends racial barriers, and many of our youths are faced with this obstacle. Absentee fathers, poverty, and sin heighten these issues.

Sadly, juvenile criminal activity seems to be growing with the increase in juvenile detention facilities. More than 500,000 American children will be incarcerated at some point this year (David Olinger- Time staff writer, *Social Issues Resource Series Youth* Vol. 4 Article 57). Youth violence continues to draw media attention as incidents mount and move closer to schools. Young people in this country are increasingly hurt by violence, feeling besieged by drug-, gang-, media-, and family-related violence that has jumped from the newspaper headlines into their backyards.

Despite public education efforts, young boys are seduced into participating in the profitable underground economy of drug trafficking. Employment for young black males aged 16 to 24 has been steadily declining since the 1970s. According to the Bureau of Labor Statistics, in 2012, only half of the black men between the ages of 20 and 24 were working. In 2012, three years after the official end of the recession, the Bureau of Labor Statistic's estimate of unemployment by age group indicated that "black men" was the only racial subgroup where the post-recession unemployment rate remained at 10 percent or above for every age category up to age 65. Often, role models in neighborhoods for young boys are, in many cases, unemployed men living the 'street life,' a life that often includes drugs. As a result, the boys of these neighborhoods are in danger of falling into a pattern of drug abuse and trafficking.

The way to avert this disaster is to give our youth positive role models, Christian role models. Also, our youth need to feel like there are options available to them, and they need decision-making and communication skills that will build their self-esteem. Street crime, specifically crime associated with drug activity, has increased dramatically over the past few years, and a monitoring/follow-up program would keep track of our youth over a long period of time.

Drug dealers are numerous and highly visible in our cities and communities. As a result, the parents of children that walk to and from school are concerned about safety. Gangs also operate in these areas, presenting young people with another negative option. At night, parks are unattended and have become the territory of drug dealers and gangs. The impact of crime, drugs, gangs, and now AIDS, on our young people is profoundly serious. The world's influences are potentially mentally, and physically, damaging, and deadly. Our society is being stripped of its young people, and it is time that we as Christian believers work to save the youth so that they may become productive citizens.

Our helping struggling should be one passion. The need for society to revisited way to rescue our youth of today is very crucial today.

Community program should be designed to motivate, and mold trouble minded into some of society's brightest individuals.

My broad ideals come from experience. I have an undergraduate degree in general psychology, so I have studied the way juveniles think and act. I also builder an institution for at-risk boys.

My reasons are very emotional for wanting to help rescue/save troubled Youth. My life has been centered around motivating teenagers to be the best they can be.

Our youngsters are growing up in an era of social media, drugs, and crime is at an all-time high in inner cities. Our society is being stripped of our young people. Young people have many obstacles to overcome. From drug trafficking, drug use, peer pressure, bullying, gang activity, to lack of opportunity.

My goal is to reach out and help some of the kids before their lives are unmanageable.

The Bible says: *"The fruit of the righteous is a tree of life and he that winneth souls is wise"* (St. Matthew 10:16). This book is an essential tool for witnessing to save our lost and hurting young people. It will train Christians to become effective witnesses for Christ. Through effective witnessing, love, compassion, and follow-up, we can honestly say that we are ***Saving Our Youth Through Outreach***.

CHAPTER 1

Effective Christian Witnessing

Let us begin by defining effective, Christian, and witness:

Effective- capable of bringing about an effect, to deliver, to bring about, accomplish.

Christian- The whole body of Christian believers; the religion stemming from the life, teaching, and death of Jesus Christ; the character or spirit of an individual.

Witness- To furnish evidence or proof such as to establish; give testimony to; provide oral or written evidence of; bear witness to; testify to.

The future of our youth depends on our ability to steer them in the right direction. The key to being effective witnesses for Christ is that we first take a personal inventory of our lives. We must identify our strengths and weaknesses. Then, we need a development plan to improve our weaknesses. A development plan can involve as little or as much as necessary. Here is an outline of a personal inventory:

I.   Strengths
II. Weaknesses
III. Improvements

Our lives are the most important witnessing tool we have. Matthew 5:16 says: *Let your light so shine before men, that they may see your good works, and glorify your Father which is in heaven.*

Because we are God's tools for reaching others, sometimes our character will be attacked. If ever there was a survey conducted concerning Christians whose reputations were attacked, the returns would probably show that at least 70% of Christians have been slandered. I have heard two noted pastors say that if your character has never been attacked as a Christian, then you are no threat to the devil. There must be some truth to this statement because the Bible tells us of how the character of the disciples and prophets was questioned because of their belief in Jesus Christ.

Let us define *character*:

> A mark, sign, distinctive quality, in accordance with a person's normal or usual qualities or traits. A mark impressed on the soul by the sacraments of baptism, confirmation, and holy orders by which the recipient is empowered to produce or receive something.

As believers, we will be lied. on, talked about, and falsely accused. Sometimes, we will be called everything but a child of God, but that should not stop us or slow us down. Our youth need to hear our witness. Proverbs 12:19, and 22 say: *The lip of truth shall be established for ever: but a lying tongue is but for a moment…. Lying lips are abomination to the Lord: but they that deal truly are his delight.* My grandfather told me that a lie will blossom and soon end, but truth will stand forever.

Even as I write this book, the Lord has shown me that many Christians are wrestling within themselves, concerned about their own Christianity and Christian walk. The following scriptures are designed to build our faith as believers. When reminiscing on years gone by, as a little girl in Illinois, I can recall my father summarizing on the three Hebrew boys, but that was the past. I can also remember him preaching on John in the book of Revelation on the vision of the new Jerusalem; that was the future. However, when daddy spoke on Paul, his writing was the present. Paul teaches us how to stand in this time and hour.

Let us begin by taking a close look at my personal favorite, the Apostle

Paul. Paul was born to a Jewish family and Roman citizenship. He was a missionary a tentmaker, and his letters to the Church became books of the New Testament. Paul said: *We are troubled on every side, yet not distressed; we are perplexed, but not in despair; Persecuted, but not forsaken; cast down, but not destroyed;* (II Corinthians 4: 8, 9). In our every day Christian walk, we will be challenged, especially when we begin to witness. We must know and realize that we have no need to be distressed or in despair; praise God we will not be forsaken or destroyed. Plus, we must always remember that although we live in natural bodies, we are not to fight in the natural, *"For though we walk in the flesh, we do not war after the flesh"* (II Corinthians 10: 3).

When we are faced with problems, we should rejoice in tribulation: *"…we glory in tribulations also: knowing that tribulation worketh patience; and patience, experience; and experience, hope:* (Romans 5: 3,4). Rejoicing in tribulation may be hard to do, but we must remember 'when praises go up, blessings come down.' After reading some of the writings of Paul, it is my hope and prayer as the author of this book that you, the reader, will gain more confidence, strength, and self-esteem, and know that God will never leave or forsake you.

When we realize that God is with us continually, Ephesians 6: 10-18 are important scriptures to believers preparing for spiritual warfare:

> *Finally, my brethren, be strong in the*
> *Lord, and in the power of his might.*
> *Put on the whole armour of God, that*
> *ye may be able to stand against the*
> *wiles of the devil. For we wrestle not against flesh and blood,*
> *but against principalities, against powers, against*
> *the rulers of the darkness of this world, against spiritual*
> *wickedness in high*
> *places. Wherefore take unto you the*
> *whole armour of God, that we may be*
> *able to withstand in the evil day, and*
> *having done all, to stand. Stand therefore, having your loins*
> *girt about with truth,*

and having on the breastplate of righteousness; And your feet
shod with
the preparation of the gospel of peace; above all, taking the
shield of faith, wherewith ye shall be able to quench all the
fiery darts of the wicked. And take the helmet of salvation,
and the sword of the spirit, which is the word of God: Praying
always with all prayer and supplication
in the spirit, and watching thereunto with
all perseverance and supplication for all
the saints;

Paul began this part of the scripture with the words, *Finally, my brethren.* This means that Paul was addressing the believers. The apostle Paul is saying that the believer gains strength by putting on *the whole armour of God.* He also talks about one of our essential tools of warfare, the word of God. Once the believer is attired with full armor, all he has to do is stand for the Lord. He/she can say, 'Lord, here I am; use me to be an *effective* witness for you.'

Knowing Our Youth.

Now, with COVID-19 Coronavirus "2020." Our entire region has been affected by the pandemic. So many have lost their jobs, their homes, their health-many who never needed help before need help now.

Youth today is facing many issues from violence to growing up too fast. The society we live in that is well into the new millennium started to recognize serious concerns that affect the youth.

ome issues have always been there but there have been new obstacles beginning to surface in the eyes of the public. With the age of social media. Some 88% of 18- to 29-year-olds indicate that they use any form of social media.

* Single Parent Households. Since the 1950s, the numbers of the single-parent households have significantly increased. ...
* Drug/Alcohol Abuse...
* Growing Up Too Fast...

* Violence in Schools...
* Bullying...
* Stress & Time Management...
* Political & Social Issues...
* Materialism...
* Education Inequality...
* Shifting Economy...

Single Parent Households

Since the 1950s, the numbers of single-parent households have significantly increased. Today, 14 million single-parent homes are responsible for 28 million children. Raising a child in itself is difficult enough, no matter whether it is a single-parent home or not, especially with tough economic conditions.

Drug/Alcohol Abuse

There have been times in history where every actor/actress in a movie was portrayed with a cigarette in hand, as smoking was considered cool. Today, about 21% of high school students admit to drug use and 41% report drinking alcohol.

Growing Up Too Fast

There was a time when kids enjoyed being kids. Today, even at the earliest of ages, some children are partaking in adult activities with serious consequences. In many places around the world children are involved in economic activities and to bear a burden of responsibility for their families.

Violence in Schools

Schools play a major role in the formation of the young person's foundation for building a life and it is reasonable to expect that the places for learning should be safe. Unfortunately, this is not always the case, as in many instances, schools can become "war zones". In the last decade 284 kids were murdered due to school violence – these were shootings, stabbings, fighting, and suicides.

Bullying is a distinctive pattern of repeatedly and deliberately harming and humiliating others, specifically those who are smaller, weaker, younger or in any way. This too is a challenge facing the youth today.

Stress & Time Management

Managing the pressure to succeed in every area of life and finding time to do it all seems to be one of the biggest challenges facing the youth today. Young people are expected to be successful, yet few of them are aware of effective time management.

Political & Social Issues

Understanding what goes on around the world and finding one's own opinion on the social and political issues, is a big challenge for the youth, who struggle to differentiate between "good" and "bad" news sources and find their way in the mud of today's world.

Materialism

We live in a society that promotes materialism and young people are taught to measure success and happiness in life based on how much stuff they have. The materialistic view on life can result in dissatisfaction when one does not have enough and can negatively affect a person's life.

Education Inequality

Different groups of young people seem to have unequal access to proper education and throughout the world, there have been continuous attempts at reforming education at all levels. Still, according to the World

Inequality Database on Education, more than 25% of children worldwide have never been to primary school.

Shifting Economy

In today's society, the open markets and globalization result in laying off workers and outsourcing work to the countries where it is cheaper. This makes it more difficult for the young people to find jobs and further complicates the already problematic lives of the youth.

During this challenging period, we remain dedicated to assisting our youth. They are the most vulnerable members of our society; they are our future.

Whatever, you can do today, you may be helping young people in your own neighborhood. Please continue.

We as believers/Christians must remain vigilant as it relates to young people. Be community minded; engaged with our community youth.

An example is, I am a volunteer with a local community at-risk youth program named Nate Comic Inc./Larry's Boys School Program. Which is fighting against systemic racism; by promoting Social Justice. This program is providing services opportunities for youth (13-18) and adults (19-24).

Mental health assessment for clients with co-occurring disorders, group, and individual therapy, treatment planning, crisis intervention, and work with the court and DCFS mandated clients in residential and outpatient settings.

Which also supervisor for methadone maintenance program - intake and assessment, group and individual therapy, billing, case management, crisis intervention, case staffing.

Their community program is effective in insuring tutors were always informed as to the most prevalent educational needs of each session, and parents and guardians were apprised of progress made each session. Mental health needs presented by parents or students were also addressed and considered during tutoring, and occasionally, additional recommendations were made for additional counseling or family therapy. Since we base the initial program on statistics regarding the communities served, gather feedback during and after servicing, and make adjustments accordingly, to meet the ongoing needs, this program is informed by evidence-based practices.

During remote learning, in addition to offering tutoring services via ZOOM, youth are able to join a support group, ZOOMCHAT, where they can sign on and talk about their concerns, perspectives on current events, the impact of racism in their lives and community, trauma, violence, etc. A similar support group is offered to parents, along with referrals and resources to other services they might need such as health care, childcare, legal assistance, employment, rental assistance, etc. One intervention that are used for both the youth and the parent support group is Real Life Heroes. It is an intervention with creative arts, activities, and psycho-education resources to engage youth and caregivers in trauma-focused services. A life storybook is included which provides a structured phased-based approach to engage youth and adults to rebuild safety hope, attachments, skills, and resources needed for trauma therapy.

Since research has shown that traumatic experiences are associated with both behavioral health and chronic physical health conditions, helping youth understand and cope with trauma will decrease their chances of repeating the cycle of violence. Individual counseling sessions are offered to parents/caregivers as well.

***Our county has incarcerated more people than any other county in the world.

The purpose of this book is to prepare you for reaching out to our lost and hurting youth, and to draw them with God's love and compassion. Let us take a look at the word *youth* and explore the theories of two noted psychologists on youth.

Youth is the condition of being young, an early period of development.

According to Levinson, there are four eras to each life. The ages they span are: 0-22 (childhood and adulthood), 17-45 (early adulthood), 40-65 (middle adulthood), 60-? (late adulthood). An adolescent is an individual who may have reached physical maturity but has not reached mental maturity. Many of the problems that young people encounter stem from the inconsistencies in their emotional, intellectual, and social development.

The teenage years are filled with new experiences, and most are faced with the turmoil of adolescence, a process called an 'identity crisis.' Noted developmental psychologist Erik H. Erikson has suggested that each adolescent must complete the task of forming an identity. Self-concepts are formed not only by what the individual believes himself to be, but by what others believe him to be. In addition, young people often attribute characteristics to themselves based on present situations. Based on these findings, it is safe to conclude that young people are very impressionable. Erikson states that if an identity crisis is not resolved, the adolescent is faced with a sense of role confusion and an inability to cope with the demands of adulthood.

When witnessing to young people, we must be mindful of the fact that they are taking on new roles and responsibilities as they move toward adulthood. We as witness for Christ must be loving, caring, and understanding, realizing that young people are yet immature and vulnerable. Also, we must consider ourselves, and remember our adolescence. Today, youth are faced with gangs, drugs, crime, teen pregnancy, and fatherless homes. Considering these things, we *must* be patient and listen to our youth.

The Lord spoke a word of prophecy into my spirit concerning the young people: There shall be a great revival, and it is coming through the youth. Just as a woman who carries a child for nine months, the church has been impregnated. The fetus within the uterus of the church is the youth. The doctor standing to deliver the baby symbolizes those of us who are 30 years of age and older. The nurses that assist in the delivery are holy angels watching from glory, waiting to help if the baby slips from the doctor's hands. The Lord said that if you are presently holy and delivered, you have a Ph. D. degree.

Satan knows that revival will come through our youth, and now he is doing everything he can to destroy them. We as the doctors must make sure that these precious babies do not slip through our fingers.

The following scriptures are key when witnessing to our youth:

> **Matthew 28: 18-20**- *And Jesus came*
> *and spake unto them, saying, All power*
> *is given unto me in heaven and in earth.*
> *Go ye therefore, and teach all nations, baptizing them in the*
> *name of the*

Father, and of the Son, and of the Holy Ghost: Teaching them to observe all
things whatsoever I have commanded
you; and, lo, I am with you always, even unto the end of the world. Amen.

John 3:16- *For God so loved the world,*
that He gave His only begotten Son, that whosoever believeth in him should not perish but have everlasting life.

Acts 3:19- *Repent ye therefore, and be converted, that your sins may be*
blotted out....

Acts 16:31-*... Believe on the Lord Jesus Christ, and thou shalt be saved, and*
thy house.

Ephesians 2:8- *For by grace are ye saved through faith; and that not of yourselves:*
it is the gift of God.

Romans 10:9- *That if thou shalt confess with thy mouth the Lord Jesus,*
and shalt believe in thine heart that God hath raised him from the dead,
thou shalt be saved.

John 17: 18-20- *As thou have sent into the world, even so have I also sent*
them into the world. And for their sakes I sanctify myself that they also
might be sanctified through the truth. Neither pray I for these alone, but
for them also which shall believe on me through their word.

I believe that there are five steps in witnessing to young people. They are:

E == Element- the weather to develop a conversation with the youth

I == Induction- tell your name, then ask their name, to personalize the conversation

C == Compliment- to develop a likeness and/or respect

E == Education- to show interest, ask what school he/she attends

W == Witness- talk about the Lord

An example of witnessing to a youth: 'Oh, it looks cloudy today. By the way, my name is Mary, and your name is? That is a nice shirt you have on. Are you in school? What school do you attend? You know, John, the Lord loves you...' As a reader, you are probably saying, 'is that all?' Yes, it is that simple!

Should a youth be reading this book and do not know Jesus Christ as his or her personal saviors say: "Lord Jesus, I know I am a sinner and need Your forgiveness. I know You died on the cross for me. I now turn from my sins and ask You to forgive me. I invite You into my heart and life. I trust You as Savior and will follow you as Lord. Thank You for saving me. Amen."

Roman 10:9 says: That if thou shalt confess with thy mouth the Lord Jesus, and shalt believe in thine heart that God hath raised him from the dead, thou shalt be saved.

You are saved!

CHAPTER 2

Essential Tools for Witnessing

Four essential tools for witnessing are a Bible, gospel tracts, a note pad, and a writing instrument. Out of the four tools mentioned above, the Bible, the word of God, is by far the most important.

A noted preacher has found that the Bible has been on the Best Seller list more than any other book because God inspired its writings, and it is profitable for doctrine, for reproof, for correction, and instruction in righteousness, that the man of God may be perfect.

Ephesians 6:17 says: *"And take the helmet of salvation and the sword of the spirit, which is the word of God...."* We also know what the Bible tells us about the sword on the spirit, which is the word of God:

> *The word of God is quick, and*
> *powerful, and sharper than any two*
> *edged sword, piercing even to the*
> *dividing asunder of soul and spirit, and*
> *of the joints and marrow, and is a*
> *discerner of the thoughts and intents of*
> *the heart.* (Hebrews 4:12)

King David said in Psalm 119:11: *Thy word have I hid in my heart, that I might not sin against thee.* We should take on the mind of David and meditate on God's word so that we develop a reservoir to fight the devil when we are attacked. Also, it will help us when we do not have a Bible on-hand. We must know the word and be able to speak encouragement to our weary, hurting youth.

My friend, the word of God should be hidden in our hearts: *Forasmuch as ye are manifestly declared to be the epistle of Christ ministered by us, written not with ink, but with the spirit of the living God; not in tables of stone, but in fleshy tables of the heart* (II Corinthians 3:3). In the word, one finds eternal life.

When we study the word of God, we find that the enemy tempted even Jesus. In St. Luke chapter 4, Jesus had just finished a forty day fast, and the devil came to tempt him:

> *And Jesus being full of the Holy*
> *Ghost returned from Jordan, and was*
> *led by the Spirit into the wilderness,*
>
> *being forty days tempted of the devil. And*
> *in those days he did eat nothing: and when they were ended,*
> *he afterward hungered.*
> *And the devil said unto him, if thou be the son of God,*
> *command this stone that it be made bread.*
>
> *And Jesus answered him, saying, It is written, that man shall*
> *not live by bread alone, but by every word of God.*
> *(Luke 4:1-4)*

The devil knew that Jesus was the Son of God, and being the trickster that he is, tried to incite him to perform miraculous acts. Instead of jumping to the devil's words, Jesus used God's word to quiet him. Jesus knew that Deuteronomy 8:3 is true: *Man, doth not live by bread only, but by every word that proceedeth out of the mouth of the Lord doth man live.* The word of God will never pass away, so we must stand on the word of God.

As ambassadors for Christ, we must encourage others to realize that accepting the Lord is the best option they have. When everything else in this world seems to crumble, St. Matthew 24:35 is true: *Heaven and earth shall pass away, but my words shall not pass away.* Without receiving the Lord, one will not have eternal life, and takes the risk of not entering the new heaven and earth. In Revelation 21:1, John says, *And I saw a new heaven and a new earth: for the first heaven and the first earth were passed away; and there was no more sea.* Isaiah 65:17 says: *For behold, I create a new heaven and a new earth, and the former shall not be remembered, nor come into mind.*

As Christian believers, we must realize that: *In the beginning was the word, and the word was with God, and the word was God* (I John 1:1). The word of God *shall not* pass away. We must have faith, and stand on the word of God, because it is the sword we use to defeat the devil. As saints of God, we must sharpen our sword.

King David knew the word of God and meditated on God's law constantly. Many times, we will not have a Bible handy when confronted by the devil. For this reason, we should be able to recall what we have read in the Bible. As witnesses, we should have the mind of David, and hid the word in our hearts: *Thy word have I hid in my heart, that I might not sin against thee* (Psalm 119:11).

We must know the word and be able to speak a word of encouragement to our weary and hurting youth. Psalm 37:31 reads: *The law of his god is in his heart; none of his steps shall slide.*

My Christian friend, the word of God should be hidden in each of our hearts with the spirit of the living God, within the fleshy tables of our heart:

> *Forasmuch as ye are manifestly declared*
> *to be the epistle of Christ ministered*
> *by us, written not with ink, but with the*
> *spirit of the living God; not in tables of*
> *stone, but in fleshy tables of the heart.*
> (II Corinthians 31:3)

Isaiah 50:4 says:
> *The Lord God hath given me a tongue*
> *of the learned, that I should know how*
> *to speak a word in season to him that*
> *is weary; he wakeneth morning by*
> *morning he wakeneth mine ear to hear*
> *as the learned.*

In my twenty-eight years of witnessing, I have found two types of youth. The first type is the listener, and the other is the seer. The listener will listen to what you have to say; the seer will ask you to show them what you are saying in the Bible. In both cases, it is vital that you carry a Bible with you.

Tracts!

Tracts, or gospel tracts, can serve as guides to the unbeliever, telling them how to live as Christians. Some tracts talk about the second coming of the Lord. Tracts are tools read at leisure, but great witnessing tools to pass out. You simply ask the person if he/she would like to read the tract; it helps to have read the information yourself, because sometime a person may ask you a question concerning the tract.

The last two essential tools are a note pad and a pen. These tools will be discussed in **Chapter 7: Follow-Up**.

CHAPTER 3

Hygiene and Nutrition

Many of us have heard it said, 'Cleanliness is next to godliness.' To be clean is to be free of dirt, germs, or impurities. David says in Psalm 51:2: *Wash me thoroughly from mine iniquity, and cleanse me from my sin*. David realized that he needed to be clean in a spiritual sense, not just in the natural. He also says in Psalm 51: *Purge me with hyssop, and I shall be clean: wash me, and I shall be whiter than snow. Create in me a clean heart, O God; and renew a right spirit within me*.

We as believers should always keep in mind that unbelievers look at outward appearance. Therefore, we should always exemplify cleanliness. Before going out to witness, we should bathe with soap and water, brush our hair and teeth, and put on fresh deodorant. Once we have cleaned our natural bodies and prayed like David in Psalm 51, we are ready to do kingdom work. It is important that we do not delay when it comes to working for the Lord, because Jesus says in John 9:4-5: *I must work the works of him that sent me, while it is day: the night cometh, when no man can work*.

Always remember that God has sent you out whenever you are witnessing. In the book of Matthew, Jesus speaks to the twelve disciples about the work before them: *Then saith he unto his disciples, The harvest truly is plenteous, but the labourers are few; Pray ye therefore the Lord of the harvest, that he will send forth labourers into his harvest* (9:37-38). Hebrews 13:21 is a prayer that God will *"Make you perfect in every good work to do his will, working in you that which is wellpleasing in his sight through Jesus Christ; to whom be glory for ever and ever. Amen."* When we have accepted the commission of God, He wont us to go forth and witness.

If you are not fasting, it is recommended that you eat a light, but healthy, breakfast during the early- or mid-morning prior to going out to witness. When you are out witnessing, you are confronting the principalities and rulers of the darkness of this world. Remember, Paul also says in II Corinthians 10:3, *"For though we walk in the flesh, we do not war after the flesh."* He also states, *"For we wrestle not against flesh and blood, but … against spiritual wickedness in high places"* (Ephesians 6:12).

Because our natural bodies house our spiritual bodies, we need to strengthen our natural bodies.

A balanced diet supplies the nutrients your body needs to work effectively. Without balanced nutrition, your body is more prone to disease, infection, fatigue, and low performance. Children who do not get enough healthy foods may face growth and developmental problems, poor academic performance, and frequent infections.

What is a Balanced Diet?

When we talk about a balanced diet it means choosing a variety of foods from the different food groups – specifically: vegetables and fruits; protein (meat, fish, eggs, beans, soy); dairy (low-fat milk, cheese, yogurt); carbohydrates (starchy foods like rice, pasta, potatoes, and bread – preferably whole grain or wholewheat varieties);, and a small quantity of healthy fats such as the unsaturated fat from olive oil. Avoid sugary drinks and foods, and foods with added saturated fat like processed meats, chips, pastries, and pies. Drink plenty of water to keep hydrated and to help your body function better.

What are the Benefits of a Balanced Diet?

1. Prevents diseases and infections. When you eat the full range of vitamins, minerals, and other nutrients you improve your immune system and your healthy diet may even help prevent diseases like cancer, heart disease, diabetes, and stroke.
2. Helps you control your weight. Most people at some point want to lose weight or gain weight – eating a balanced diet helps you control your weight and maintain it over time. It is not feasible to

be on a weight-loss diet forever – a balanced diet is the only way to healthily control your weight in the long term.

3. Improves your mental health. Getting the right mix of nutrients can help to ease symptoms of depression and anxiety – looking after yourself by eating well is essential as you take steps to good mental health.

4. Good for growth. A balanced diet is crucial for children and adolescents. As the body grows it is important to receive the right nutrients so that cells are built and maintained, and the body grows at the right pace.

5. Better skin and hair. A healthy balanced diet also improves your looks. Eating well contributes to healthy skin and hair and a "glow" that makes you look younger.

Saints and Believers no I am not a nutritionist and yes consult your physician/doctor before starting new diet. We should eat healthy foods and cook with herbs. For breakfast, energy foods are beneficial. We should limit salty, sweet, and greasy foods. A small portion of meat from the recommended meat list (below) is approved with breakfast. According to the Mississippi State Department of Health (1984), the following breakfast menu is suggested:

MEAT LIST- CHOOSE ONE
Egg (no fat added)- 1 whole: *no more than three per week
Egg white or substitute- ¼ cup
Lean ham- 1 ounce
Cottage cheese- ¼ cup

STARCH/ BREAD LIST- CHOOSE ONE
All bran- 1/3 cup
Corn bran 1/2 cup
Flakes (1 ounce)- 1 cup
Oatmeal (cooked)- ½ cup
Grits (cooked)- ½ cup
Bread/ toast- 1 slice

FRUIT LIST- CHOOSE ONE
Orange- 1 small
Strawberries- 1 ¼ cup
Prunes- 3 medium
Raisins- 2 tablespoons
Orange juice- ½ cup
Banana- ½ 9-inch

FAT LIST- CHOOSE ONE
Margarine- 1 teaspoon
Corn oil- 1 teaspoon
Bacon- 1 strip

MILK LIST- CHOOSE ONE
Skim milk- 1 cup
Plain low-fat yogurt- 1 cup
Skim evaporated milk- ½ cup
Nonfat dry milk- 1/3 cup

FREE FOODS
Coffee, nothing added
Tea, unsweetened
Diet drinks

This breakfast list is designed to assist with breakfast selections. If you eat better, you will feel better. In many cases, eating before you go witnessing will lessen the likelihood of being hungry while out. However, if the Lord leads you to fast, do what Jesus commands in St. Matthew 6:16-18:

> *Moreover, when ye fast, be not, as*
> *the hypocrites, of a sad countenance:*
> *for they disfigure their faces, that they*
> *may appear unto men to fast. Verily I*
> *say unto you, they have their reward.*

But thou when thou fasteh, anoint thine head, and wash thy face; That thou
appear not unto men to fast, but unto
thy Father, which is in secret: and thy Father which seeth in
secret shall reward thee openly.

Jesus is saying that it is good to fast, but we should not look like we are doing it under duress. We should present ourselves in a positive way.

CHAPTER 4

Pairing (two by two)

There is a great significance in pairing. Where there is unity, there is strength; whenever believers' pair up, there is great power. St. Matthew 18:19-20. tells us:

> *Again I say unto you, that if two of you*
> *shall agree on earth as touching any*
> *thing that they shall ask, it shall be done*
> *for them of my Father which is in heaven.*
>
> *For where two or three are gathered together in my name,*
> *there am I in the*
> *midst of them.*

There is power when believers come together with one mind, one soul, and one purpose.

Jesus Christ sent the disciples out two-by-two: *"and when they drew nigh unto Jerusalem, and were come to Bethphage, unto the mount of Olives, then sent Jesus two disciples"* (Matthew 21:1). Jesus sent the disciples on a mission into a village. Even today, Jesus is sending believers to the field. The mission, today, is to go into a town, city, state, or country, to find unbelievers (youths) who are tied up in sin and bring them to Jesus. St. Mark 6:7 says, *"And he called unto him, the twelve, and began to send them forth by two and two; and gave them power over unclean spirits;"*

Ecclesiastes also tells us that two are better than one. If one falls, the other will lift him up.

> *Two are better than one; because they*
> *have a good reward for their labor.*
> *For if they fall, the one will lift up his fellow: but woe to him*
> *that is alone*
> *when he falleth; for he hath not another*
> *to help him up. Again, if two lie*
> *together, then have they heat: but how*
> *can one be warm alone? And if one*
> *prevail against hi m two shall withstand him; and a threefold*
> *cord is not quickly broken.* (4:9-11)

Christian friends, there is great power when we pair together. In the book of Deuteronomy, we find that with the Lord's help, one will chase a thousand, and two will put ten thousand to flight: *How should one chase a thousand, and two put ten thousand to flight, except their Rock had sold them, and the Lord had shut them up?* (32:30). It is time that we take the city we live in and bring our youth to Christ. Then we as Christians can re-establish the proper Christian values, morals, love, and familial bonds.

Always remember that we should be on one accord when speaking to non-believers. Amos 3:3 say, *"Can two walk together, except they be agreed?"* We have been commanded to witness to the lost (our lost youth). My friend, is God sending you forth as a laborer? Will you answer the call of God?

Jesus said that we must pray to the Lord to send forth laborers. Will you touch and agree with me in prayer for laborers in the harvest? Matthew 21:22 says: *And all things, whatsoever ye shall ask in prayer, believing, ye shall receive.* John 14:13 reads: *And whatsoever ye shall ask in my name, that will I do, that the Father may be glorified in the Son.* Finally, Matthew 7:7 says: *Ask and it shall be given you; seek, and ye find; knock, and it shall be opened unto you.* The letter **A** is for **Ask**, **S** is for **Seek**, and **K** is for **Knock**. These letters spell **ASK**.

While one believer is witnessing/ speaking to the youth, the other believer should be praying and asking the Lord to break strongholds and save. We should keep II Corinthians 10: 3-4 in mind: *For though we walk in the flesh, we do not war after the flesh: (For the weapons of our warfare are not carnal, but mighty through God to the pulling down of strongholds:).* We have been commanded by our Lord and Saviour to go forth and witness to the lost.

Do you recall the resurrection of Christ in the book of St. Matthew:

> *And Jesus came and spake unto them,*
> *saying, All power is given unto me in*
> *heaven and in earth.*
>
> *Go ye therefore, and teach all nations, baptizing them in the*
> *name of the Father, and of the Son, and of the Holy Ghost:*
> *Teaching them to observe all things whatsoever I have*
> *commanded you: and,*
> *lo, I am with you alway, even unto the*
> *end of the world. Amen.* (28:18-20)

CHAPTER 5

Love

Our young people today are faced with many obstacles. For this reason, we should continue to show love. Love plays an especially important role when witnessing to young people and unbelievers. Black children endure constant media attacks. They are often portrayed as violent criminals, drug dealers, and on welfare. We as believers must rise up and say, 'no more attacks on our young people.' We must begin by showing our young men a better lifestyle, a Christian lifestyle.

LOVE is the key - Saints and believers we should remember the interface between racism/classism and attendant economic and social disadvantages is the key to understanding the underachievement of African American children. African Americans have been exposed to generations of legal and illegal measures to deny them basic rights. From slavery to Jim Crow and to today's housing, health care, and voting inequities, the African American community has endured unrelenting racism that begins at an early age. Love is a major platform to reach each other.

We love the people but hate the sin that has overtaken their lives. We have been commanded to love. Jesus said:

> *thou shalt love the Lord thy God with*
> *all thy heart, and with all thy soul,*
> *and with all thy mind. This is the first*
> *and great commandment. And the*

second is like unto the first: thou shalt
love thy neighbor as thyself. On these
two commandments hang all the law
and the prophets. (Matthew 22:37-40)

Why should we love? Because we represent God as His ambassadors. What does the Bible say about the love of God? Read I John 4: 7-8.

According to a study, the US incarceration

On December 31, 2009, state and federal correctional authorities had jurisdiction over 1,613,740 prisoners, an increase of 3,981 prisoners from yearend 2008. The United States is the world's leader in incarceration with 2.2 million people currently in the nation's prisons and jails — a 500% increase over the last forty years. Changes in sentencing law and policy, not changes in crime rates, explain most of this increase. These trends have resulted in prison overcrowding and fiscal burdens on states to accommodate a rapidly expanding penal system, despite increasing evidence that large-scale incarceration is not an effective means of achieving public safety.

Another study also concluded that the black men in prisons and jails are more than the black men enrolled in institutions of higher learning.

The disproportionate incarceration of minority populations may have an adverse impact on the generalizability of clinical research. In 2009, 40 percent of the men and women who were incarcerated were black; 3 more than one-third of black men are incarcerated at some point in their lives. Under these circumstances, the results of longitudinal studies may fail to represent accurately the experience of black populations and may bias estimates of racial disparities by either excluding people in jail or prison or discontinuing longitudinal follow-up at the time of incarceration. Society says incarcerate them; we as believers say save them, educate them.

We must let our light shine to this dying generation of young people. The Bible says in Matthew 5:16, *"Let your light so shine before men, that they may see your good works, and glorify your Father which is in heaven."* The Bible is telling us to be positive examples; this is a sure way to draw others. The Bible is letting us know that salvation and deliverance will come. Knowing this, we must throw our love and our light to our youth, showing them that we are serious about our lives as Christians. As believers, we should let our light shine before men (youth), that they may see our good works, and glorify our Father which is in heaven.

We as Christians should be positive role models. I can think of no other person than Jesus Christ to exemplify love, positivity, and holiness. Jesus is the best role model one can have. Jesus considered us his friends, and he laid down his life for us. John 15:13 says *"Greater love hath no man than this, that a man lay down his life for a friend."*

Jesus considered us as friends; He laid down His life for us. Can any of us think of a friend in this day and age who would do that? I, for one, cannot think of anyone. Jesus loves all of us with an everlasting love.

Do you recall in St. Mark the great commandment concerning love:

> *And Jesus answered him, The first of*
> *all the commandments is, Hear, O*
> *Israel; the Lord our God is one Lord:*
>
> *And thou shalt love the Lord thy*
> *God with all thy heart, and with all*
> *thy soul, and with all thy mind, and*
> *with all thy strength: this is the first*
> *commandment.*
>
> *And the second is like, namely this,*
> *Thou shalt love thy neighbor as thyself. There is none other*
> *commandment*
> *greater than these.* (12:29-31)

We as believers should recognize the importance of the word *Christian*. To be a Christian means to be Christ-like. We should be careful to live up to the title and the commandments of God. As Christians, we have an obligation to bring as many to Christ as we can. The book of St. John has a lot to say about love and its importance in our lives. John 15:12 says: *This is my commandment, that ye love one another, as I have loved you.* Therefore, it is through our witness that we can show love and tell others that someone cares. In John 13:34, we find a similar commandment: *A new commandment I give unto you, that ye love one another; as I have loved you, that ye also love one another.* Surely, we can do this because we were drawn by love*: "The lord hath appeared of old unto me, saying, Yea, I have loved thee with an everlasting love: therefore with lovingkindness have I drawn thee"* (Jeremiah 31:3).

Are you as a Christian living up to the commandments of Christ? Remember: *But God commendeth His love toward us, in that, while we were yet sinners, Christ died for us* (Romans 5:8). Because of this, we as believers ought to thank God every day for His love that means so much. God has drawn each of us with His loving kindness; likewise, we will draw our youth to Christ by showing them love. Most importantly, we as believers must exhibit the fruits of the spirit according to Galatians 5:22-23: *"But the fruit of the spirit is love, joy, peace, longsuffering, gentleness, goodness, faith, meekness, temperance: against such there is no law."*

Love plays a vital role in salvation. When we were in sin, the Lord extended His love to us and by His grace and mercy we have the opportunity to repent for our wrongdoings. In I John 1:9, we come to know that *if we confess our sins, he is faithful and just to forgive us our sins, and to cleanse us from all unrighteousness.*

As we witness to the youth of today, we must let them know that regardless of the sins they have committed, there is hope for them. In Isaiah 1:18, The Lord is pleading for us to receive His love: *Come now, and let us reason together, saith the Lord: though your sins be as scarlet, they shall be as white as snow; though they be red like crimson, they shall be as wool.* This scripture should reassure young people of God's love and forgiveness. Many times, young people feel like they are beyond forgiveness because of the sins they have committed. They may feel like there is no hope for them, or like they are not good enough to be saved. Yet we need to show them that we have an answer! Our youth must come to know that all they must do is ask Jesus Christ into their hearts. If they will act according to Romans 10:9 that says: *That if thou shalt confess with thy mouth the Lord Jesus, and shalt believe in thine heart that God hath raised him from the dead, thou shalt be saved,* their sins will be forgiven, and they will be saved. When a young person receives salvation, he/she has confessed the sin in his/her life and has asked the Lord to come into his/her life forever. Romans 10:10 reads: *For with the heart man believeth unto righteousness; and with the mouth confession is made unto salvation.* Tell the youth that they are saved by faith, and this act of faith pleases the Lord.

I once heard a fictional story by a noted pastor tell a story about a man named Johnny Brown. An angel made known that Johnny Brown was born today, and it was acknowledged by Yahweh, that's good. The second time the angel reported to Yahweh, Johnny Brown took his first step today an acknowledged by Yahweh that's good. Later, the angel reported to Yahweh about Johnny Brown's first day of kindergarten, his graduation from elementary school, his sixteenth birthday, and his graduation from high school.

But on the seventh time, when the angel made known that Johnny got saved on today, it was acknowledged with excitement by Yahweh, Johnny got saved! Bring out the stringed instruments, let us rejoice!

Luke 15:6 (KJV)And when he cometh home, he calleth together his friends and neighbours, saying unto them, Rejoice with me; for I have found my sheep which was lost.

In St. Luke, one will see that the heavens rejoice over the salvation of one soul:

> *I say unto you, that likewise joy shall*
> *be in heaven over one sinner that*
> *repenteth, more than over ninety and*
> *nine just persons, which need no*
> *repentance... Likewise, I say unto you,*
> *there is joy in the presence of the angels*
> *of God over one sinner that repenteth.*
> (15:7, 10)

Our youth must realize that they are important to God, and that just like in the story, the Lord and the angels are excited when they leave their lives of sin.

CHAPTER 6

Compassion

Compassion is important when witnessing to unbelievers. As Christians, we must understand that sinners and unbelievers are hurting and suffering, being weak to the sin that binds them. Fortunately, God is compassionate. In Psalm 78:38, we see God dealing with children of disobedience: *But he, being full of compassion, forgave their iniquity, and destroyed them not: yea, many a time turned he his anger away, and did not stir up all his wrath.* If our heavenly Father can be compassionate and forgive iniquity, so can we.

The book of Psalms contains many scriptures regarding the Lord's compassion:

> **Psalm 86:15**- *But thou, O Lord, art a*
> *God full of compassion, and gracious, longsuffering, and*
> *plenteous in mercy*
> *and truth.*
> **Psalm 111:4**- *He hath made his*
> *wonderful works to be remembered:*
> *the Lord is gracious and full of*
> *compassion.*
> **Psalm 112:4**- *Unto the upright there*
> *ariseth light in darkness: he is*
> *gracious, and full of compassion, and righteousness.*

When witnessing to our youth, we must remember that we are a light to this dark world (Matthew 5:14). Therefore, we must have a sense of compassion for each other. Our youth are looking for positive examples, and we should strive to live according to Matthew 5:16: *Let your light so shine before men, that they may see your good works, and glorify your Father which is in heaven.* If we are to be effective witnesses, we must be like Jesus. In John 8:12, Jesus said, *I am the light of the world: he that followeth me shall not walk in darkness but shall have the light of life.* Jesus is the light of the world, and those who accept Christ no longer walk in darkness, but in light.

> St. John 12:35 reads:
> *Then Jesus said unto them, Yet a little while is the light with you. Walk while ye have the light, lest darkness come upon you: for he that walketh in darkness knoweth not whither he goeth.*

While you have light, believe in the light, that you may be the children of light. These things spake Jesus and departed and did hide himself from them.

In order to be a light to this dark world, we must have compassion, especially to our lost and hurting youth. If we cannot show compassion, how can we say that the love of God is in us? I John 3:17 says: *But whoso hath this world's good, and seeth his brother in need, and shutteth up his bowels of compassion from him, how dwelleth the love of God in him?*

We as Christians must have compassion on our brethren. We should live according to I Peter 3:8 that says: *Finally, be ye all of one mind, having compassion one of another, love as brethren, be pitiful, be courteous.*

Even our heavenly Father has compassion. In the book of Deuteronomy, we find:

> *That then the Lord thy God will turn thy captivity, and have compassion upon thee, and will return and gather thee from all the nations, whither the Lord thy God hath scattered thee.*
> (30:3)

In Romans 9:15, it is recorded that the Lord "*saith unto Moses, I will have mercy on whom I will have mercy, and I will have compassion on whom I will have compassion.* Psalm 145:8 clearly states that the Lord is full of compassion: *The Lord is gracious, and full of compassion; slow to anger, and of great mercy.*

When you are out witnessing and non-believer refuses to listen or tries to overtalk you, be slow to anger and smile. When they have finished, show them the scriptures you are speaking about so that they may understand.

Remember the challenge facing black youth and or youth of color today.

Compassion MATTERS - Sadly rarely black youth get media attention unless they commit a crime or are killed.

A survey conducted by telephone in February 2014 by Lester & Associates, also found that 88 percent of respondents are "very satisfied" or "somewhat satisfied" with their quality of life. Despite the many problems and challenges African Americans face in 2014, they display the same strength and resilience that have characterized their 400-year struggle in America. Most express high levels of satisfaction with their lives in general and in the aggregate, they have an estimated buying power of over $1 trillion dollars annually. Yet at the same time, many problems persist.

Specifically, the poll also found that:

*   74% think society is not doing enough to support young men and boys of color.
*   Almost two-thirds say they are better off financially than they were five years ago, but 82% are concerned that Whites still make more than Blacks for doing the same jobs.
*   52% see the media's portrayal of African Americans as generally negative.
*   60% of respondents agree we are making progress in providing access to health care.
*   Almost 1/3 are concerned that their children are not getting a quality education.
*   44% said they knew someone who had committed suicide or was killed.

* Seventy-four percent say efforts to reduce crime and violence in their neighborhood is losing ground or staying the same.
* 30% said "improving the creating more jobs/good paying jobs" is a top issue of concern.

Five (5) Common Problems Faced by African Americans today:

1. Lack of family structure: According to a 2002 study, 70% of all African American children were illegitimate and that number rose from 23.6% back in 1963 because that was the year when welfare became a right according to the constitution, which made having husbands redundant. Too many African American families grow up without a father figure in the house, which often leads to psychological issues later in life.
2. Dangerous cities have high African American Populations: Dangerous cities like Oakland, Cleveland, Baltimore, and Detroit where gang violence and crime are an everyday occurrence has a high population of African American people who live under the government of Democrats.
3. High abortion rates: It is estimated that 30% of all abortions in the country are done by African American women. This heightened loss of uncounted lives percolates to reduce respect for life and has played its role in decreasing civility with which people treat each other.
4. The victim mindset: Nothing holds an African American back more than seeing themselves as a victim who sees everything as someone else's fault without taking the deserved responsibility to such a significant degree that their victim status becomes their collective identity.
5. African Americans make up a sizable portion of prisoners: Studies infer that 52% of homicides are committed by African American individuals. Due to this high incarceration rate, every 1 in 9 African American children you pass on the sidewalk may have or might have had a parent in prison. Due to the greater likelihood of African Americans being incarcerated, their social upbringing and family support have taken the toll.

As believers, we must always have mercy on our youth and show kindness to them. Remember that we were once lost and bound to sin, until we accepted God's love, compassion, and mercy. Ephesians 2:4 (KJV) reads: We should let the youth know that God's goodness and mercy is everlasting: *But God, who is rich in mercy, for his great love wherewith he loved us...*

The Old Testament is full of references to God's mercy:
Psalm 100:5- *For the Lord is good, his mercy is everlasting, and His truth endureth to all generations.*
I Chronicles 16:34- O *give thanks unto The Lord, for he is good; for his Mercy endureth forever.*
Psalm 106:1- *Praise ye the Lord, O give thanks unto the Lord; for he is good: for his mercy endureth forever.*

My Christian friends, it is my opinion that the Lord's mercy and compassion are inter-connected with one another. Jesus Himself was moved with compassion in the book of St. Matthew:

But when he saw the multitudes, he Was moved with compassion on them, because they fainted, and were scattered abroad, as sheep having no shepherd.
Then saith he unto his disciples, The Harvest truly is plenteous, but the Laborers are few;

Pray ye therefore the Lord of the Harvest, that he will send forth Laborers into his harvest.
(9:36-38)

In this scripture, Jesus is stressing the fact that people have fainted and scattered due to a shortage of shepherds (pastors). There are so many souls in this world that need God's salvation. Will you pray? Will you be one of the laborers?

Do you remember the story about the woman of Canaan in St Matthew? Let us take a look at this story:

Then Jesus went thence, and departed into the coasts of Tyre and Sidon.

And, behold, a woman of Canaan came out of the same coasts and saying, have mercy on me, O Lord thou son of David; my daughter is grievously vexed with a devil.

But he answered her not a word. And his disciples came and besought him, saying, Send her away; for she crieth after us.

But he answered and said, I am not sent but unto the lost sheep of Israel.

Then she came and worshipped him, saying, Lord, help me.

But he answered and said, It is not meet to take the children's bread, and cast it to the dogs.

And she said, Truth, Lord: yet the dogs eat of the crumbs which fall from their masters' table.

Then Jesus answered and said unto her, O woman, great is thy faith: be it unto thee even as thou wilt. And her daughter was made whole from that very hour. (15:21-28)

The Canaanite woman needed what Jesus had, and she persisted until Jesus granted her request. This woman had great faith and she was humble. Not too many people would accept being called a dog. This scripture concludes with Jesus' mercy and compassion.

I believe that this Canaanite woman thought within her heart what Hebrews 4:15-16 says:

> *For we have not an high priest which*
> *cannot be touched by the feeling of*
> *our infirmities; but was in all points*
> *tempted like we are, yet without sin.*
>
> *Let us therefore come boldly to the*
> *throne of grace, that we might obtain*
> *mercy, and find grace to help in time*
> *of need.*

Oh, Praise God! Do you remember the year, month, week, day, hour, second within the minute that you, being bound to sin, came boldly to the throne of grace, and obtained salvation? Since you have a testimony, go forth and testify to unbelievers. In turn, they may come boldly to the throne of grace and obtain grace, compassion, and salvation in **Jesus Christ!**

CHAPTER 7

Follow-up

When out witnessing, after a person accepts Christ as personal Savior, the next step is follow-up. Let us begin by defining the word *follow*: to go after or along, to happen after, conform to, learn from, or understand. At this point in witnessing, it is necessary to have a note pad and a pen (two essentials listed in Chapter 2) to obtain contact information for the new souls. Whenever a person accepts Christ, he/she is a new creature: *Therefore if any man be in Christ he is a new creature: old things are passed away; behold, all things are become new* (II Corinthians 5:17).

The moment a young person accepts Christ as personal Savior, every wrongdoing committed in their life is forgiven. I John 2:12 says: *I write unto you, little children, because your sins are forgiven you for his name's sake.* There is therefore now no condemnation in Christ. I John 1:7 affirms this fact when it says: *But if we walk in the light, as he is in the light, we have fellowship one with another, and the blood of Jesus Christ his son cleanseth us from all sin.* If God forgave our sins, even we as Christians must forgive. II Corinthians 2:10 reads: *To whom ye forgive anything, I forgave also: for if I forgave any thing, to whom I forgave it, for your sake forgave I it in the person of Christ;*

Our Lord and Savior Jesus Christ told Peter that we should forgive our brother seventy times seven:

> *Then came Peter to him, and said, Lord,*
> *how oft shall my brother sin against me,*
> *and I forgive him? Till seven times?*

Jesus said unto him, I say not unto thee, until seven times;
but, until seventy
times seven. (Matthew 18:21-22)

In keeping with the above scriptures, we must keep in mind that: *For if ye forgive men their trespasses, your heavenly Father will also forgive you.* Matthew 6:14 (KJV)

We must forgive to gain God's forgiveness.

The moment a youth accepts Christ, God forgives all past sins. The individual is reborn, and his/her sins are blotted out. Acts 3:19 says: *Repent ye therefore, and be converted, that your sins may be blotted out, when the times of refreshing shall come from the presence of the Lord;* The youth become spiritually reborn.

Recall the story of Nicodemus in the book of John. As an educator in Israel, even he learned of rebirth from Jesus:

Jesus answered and said unto him,
Verily, verily, I say unto thee, except
a man be born again, he cannot see
the kingdom of God.

Nicodemus saith unto him, How can a
man be born when he is old? Can he
enter the second time into his mother's womb, and be born?

Jesus answered, verily, verily, I say
unto thee, except a man be born of
water and of the spirit, he cannot enter
into the kingdom of God. (John 3:3-5)

Jesus tells Nicodemus about spiritual birth. Likewise, the youth experience a spiritual birth. He/she becomes a baby again, a baby in Christ.

This is the new birth, the spiritual birth. In this stage, the individual needs to be taught the ways of God and the Church. That is why it is especially important that proper follow-up be established and practiced until the youth reaches maturity in Christ.

This will show the youth your love and concern as a Christian. Even

Jesus Christ called the disciples to follow Him, so that they could be taught the ways of God:

> *From that, Jesus began to preach, and*
> *to say, Repent: for the kingdom of*
> *heaven is at hand.*
>
> *And Jesus, walking by the sea of*
> *Galilee saw two brethren, Simon*
> *called Peter, and Andrew his brother,*
> *casting a net into the sea: for they*
> *were fishers.*
>
> *And he saith unto them, Follow me,*
> *and I will make you fishers of men.*
>
> *And they straightway left their nets,*
> *and followed him.* (Matthew 4:17-20)

The scripture goes on to say that Jesus called two more brethren, James and John, as they were mending their nets: *And they immediately left the ship and their father and followed him* (4:22).

The disciples gave up their ways to follow Jesus. They knew that Jesus would not harm them. He stood for righteousness and goodness, so they followed Him. I Peter 3:13 reads: *And who will harm you, if ye be followers of that which is good.*

Since the disciples followed Jesus with their hearts, Jesus said in Matthew 19:28:

> *And Jesus said unto them, verily I*
> *say unto you, that ye which have*
> *followed me, in the regeneration*
> *when the son of man shall sit on the*
> *throne of His glory, ye also shall*
> *sit upon twelve thrones, judging the*
> *twelve tribes of Israel.*

My friend, after Jesus taught the disciples the way of the Lord, they did follow-up work with the people they witnessed to and came in contact with.

An example of follow-up can be found in the book of John. Jesus healed a man who was unable to walk:

> *For an angel went down at a certain*
> *Season into the pool, and troubled*
> *the water: whosoever then first after*
> *the troubling of the water stepped in*
> *was made whole of whatsoever*
> *disease they had.*
>
> *And a certain man was there,*
> *which had an infirmity thirty and*
> *eight years.*
>
> *When Jesus saw him lie, and knew*
> *that he had been a long time case,*
> *He saith unto him, Wilt thou be*
> *made whole?*
>
> *The impotent man answered him, sir,*
> *I have no man, when the water is*
> *troubled, to put me into the pool: but*
> *while I was coming, another steppeth*
> *down before me.*
>
> *Jesus saith unto him, Rise, take up thy*
> *Bed, and walk.* (John 5:4-8).

The same passage of scripture says: *Afterward, Jesus findeth him in the temple, and said unto him, Behold, thou art made whole: sin no more, lest a worse thing come unto thee (14).* Jesus first healed the man of his illness, then He followed up with him, warning him to put away his life of sin

Jesus showed another example of follow-up in Matthew 9:18-19, & 9: 23-25:

While he spake these things unto
them, behold, there came a certain
ruler, and worshipped him, saying,
my daughter is even now dead:
but come and lay thy hand on
her, and she shall live.

And Jesus arose, and followed
him, and so did his disciples.

And when Jesus came into the
rulers house, and saw the
minstrels and the people making
a noise,

He said unto them, Give place:
for the maid is not dead, but
sleepeth. And they laughed him
to scorn.

But when they were put forth,
he went in, and took her by the
hand, and the maid arose.

It may have seemed like Jesus was not concerned by the situation, but in the end, He went to the trouble and worked out the problem. Many times, we will have to go into a person's home and minister to them. That is why pairing (Chapter 4) is so important. We should never go alone, for even Jesus had company with the disciples. After reviewing the works of Jesus while He was on earth, certainly, there is plenty of follow-up to be done.

We, too, as Christians must follow Jesus' example. We should go to sinners and unbeliever's homes and minister the gospel to them.

I can recall, as a young woman in high school, Maywood, Illinois, in the late 1970's. One Sunday morning at Miracle Revival Center, Bishop Willie J. Chambliss got up to deliver his sermon, and said,' I'm sending you out two-by-two (one person who knows the word of God and one who prays) to minister outdoors and go door-to-door in order to bring the sinners and unbelievers back with you at 12 noon.' When we returned to the church, it was filled to capacity with no standing room. The experience had a profound effect on my life. Praise God for leaders who obey the voice of the Lord.

It is my hope and prayer that everyone who reads this book will answer the call of Christ, the call of outreach ministry. Jesus is sending believers on a mission. The mission is to go into villages, towns, cities, states, and countries to identify those who do not know Jesus as their savior. Our task is not easy, but with Jesus as our strength, we can prevent a number of our youth from continuing in sin and heading towards eternal damnation and destruction. Our society is being stripped of our young people. It is time to save them, rescue them from life turbulence and in so doing, save our future.

I pray that after reading this book, every reader will say: **'Here I am Lord, send me!'**

Let us Believe GOD Together
For Souls

I pray that after reading this book, every reader will say: **"Here I am Lord, send me."**

For Jesus said St. Luke 10:2 say: "Therefore said he unto them, The harvest truly is great, but the labourers are few: pray ye therefore the Lord of the harvest, that he would send forth labourers in to his harvest."

Prayer Requests

Mary, please pray for the needs I have written below.

_____

_____

I would like to plant a faith-seed/gift $_____
For youth soul's outreach. This will enable us to give copies of this book to a youth that is less fortunate than our salves. Will you give on today to help save a child? **A youth!**

Mail to: Outreach Saving Our Youth c/o Dr. Mary "May" Larry, Ph.D. P.O. Box 13 Maywood, IL. 60153.
And or give by way of CASH APP at: **$MaryMayLarry**
Charitable contribution is tax exempt. Donate online to the Larry's Boys School Program Organizations at: **https://larrysboysschoolprogram.com/**

NOTES:

THANK YOU FOR GIVING AND FOR READING MY BOOK: OUTREACH SAVING OUR YOUTH!

Dr. Mary "May" Larry, Ph.D.
Author

Printed in the United States
By Bookmasters